Blair House has stood facing the White House for over 150 years, its windows granting a view of the most important events in our nation's capital. More than just the President's Guest House, the Blair House is the Guest House of the Nation. As such, it reflects the history and traditions that have made America what it is today.

We know that future chiefs of state, heads of government, and other distinguished visitors who come to our country from abroad will find here a home away from home, one which provides the finest of American hospitality. It is our hope that they will take back to their own countries the warmest memories of their stay.

The Blair House Restoration Fund

(Page 1) *Blair House Front Entrance.*
(Page 2) *Blair House.*
(Pages 4-5) *Blair House Dining Room.*
(Pages 6-7) *Dillon Room.*
(Above) *Curio Room.*

Produced by Thomasson-Grant, Inc., Charlottesville, Virginia: Frank L. Thomasson III and John F. Grant, Directors; C. Douglas Elliott, Product Development; Carolyn M. Clark, Creative Director; Mary Alice Parsons, Art Director; Hoke Perkins, Senior Editor; Jim Gibson, Production Manager.

Text by Marlene Elizabeth Heck
Photography by Kari Haavisto, Hickey-Robertson, Mary E. Nichols, and John F. Grant

Editorial Consultant: Selwa Roosevelt
Designed by Carolyn F. Weary
Edited by Elizabeth L. T. Brown
Printed in the United States by Hoechstetter Printing, Inc.
95 94 93 92 91 90 89   5 4 3 2 1

Library of Congress Cataloging-in-Publication Data
Blair House, the president's guest house / interior decorators, Mario Buatta and Mark Hampton; [text by Marlene Elizabeth Heck; photography by Karl Haavisto . . . et al.].
    p.   cm.
    ISBN 0-934738-48-3
    1. Blair House (Washington, D.C.)—Pictorial works. 2. Interior decoration—Washington (D.C.)—Pictorial works. 3. Washington (D.C.)—Buildings, structures, etc.—Pictorial works. I. Buatta, Mario. II. Hampton, Mark. III. Heck, Marlene Elizabeth.
IV. Haavisto, Kari.
F204.B5B57 1989
975.3—dc19   88-72129
                                                  CIP

BLAIR HOUSE

The President's Guest House

Interior Decorators
Mario Buatta and Mark Hampton

Capitol dome.

*W*ashington possesses a beauty and dignity that belie its youth. The scale, number, and architectural inspiration of the buildings that flank its wide avenues give the city—not yet 200 years old—the appearance and ambience of a classical national capital. Washington's radiating streets, monuments, vistas, and parklands compose a grandeur not repeated in any other American city, one that reflects the ideals and ambitions of the nation as well as those of its first president, George Washington, and his designer, the French military engineer Major Pierre Charles L'Enfant. Their plan, far beyond what the country needed or could afford at the time, was the product of their determination to create a capital, as L'Enfant wrote, "beautiful above what may be imagined," even if it meant doing so in the midst of a wilderness.

By 1800, barely a decade after its creation, Washington's slow, unsure development already had begun to disappoint its founders. George Washington's and Pierre Charles L'Enfant's vision of a glorious city stretched across broad avenues, rivaling the capitals of the ancient world, was more than a century in the making.

In the fall of 1790, George Washington left Philadelphia to execute one of the most politically charged duties of his presidency: the selection of the site for the new American capital. The place he chose along the marshy shores of the Potomac River had been the hunting grounds of Algonquin Indians just a century before and was still only sparsely populated. The land was marked by little more than the paths over which tobacco traders carted their leaf to market at Alexandria and Georgetown. Despite the unfavorable appearance of the new capital's location, the president from the beginning conceived it in broad, majestic terms, comparing the scope of his plan to that of London, then the world's premier city.

Washington turned the project over to designer Pierre Charles L'Enfant the following spring. Demonstrating his understanding of the city's symbolic role as the embodiment of the new republic's ideals and permanence, L'Enfant, in his earliest correspondence with Washington, urged the president to spare no effort to ensure the creation of a noble and dignified city. In later progress reports, L'Enfant repeatedly used the words "grand" and "magnificent" to describe the city he was crafting.

Less than six months after he began, L'Enfant completed his urban scheme. The engineer, who grew up at the Palace of Versailles and later studied in Paris, incorporated the formality and impressive vistas of French gardens and Parisian boulevards into his plan. His elaborate, gridlike design of streets overlaid by circles and broad, diagonal avenues displayed a complexity and scale more reminiscent of European towns than of the other planned American cities—Alexandria, Williamsburg, Savannah, Philadelphia, and Annapolis—that preceded it.

View of the City of Washington. *T. Moore, 1838.*

For the nation's most important building, the Capitol, L'Enfant reserved the city's highest spot, then known as Jenkin's Hill. He described the site as "a pedestal waiting for a superstructure," and proposed to enhance its natural beauty by creating a waterfall that would cascade into a Grand Canal flowing through the city's center. L'Enfant also proposed a palatial home for the president, nearly five times larger than the present White House. However, because the protracted war for independence from Britain had exhausted the country's financial resources and its taste for monarchial pretensions, L'Enfant's structure, like the Capitol cascade, the Grand Canal, and numerous other elements in his scheme, was never built.

L'Enfant's aspirations for the capital city exceeded those of Washington, who was acutely aware of the nation's empty treasury.

But the president, recognizing the design's beauty and intelligence, never voiced any objection. L'Enfant's active role ended in February 1792 when the president was forced to dismiss the strong-willed designer who had repeatedly refused to comply with the wishes of the district commissioners. Later that year, construction on the City of Washington in the Territory of Columbia commenced without L'Enfant's direction, but according to his design.

Long before November 1800 when Congress opened its first session in Washington, curious Europeans and Americans journeyed for a look at the new federal city. Many had heard the widely circulated stories of an elegant city rising along the Potomac River. Others had seen a beautiful map of radiating boulevards and magnificent buildings, distributed by the young government to spur interest and development in the capital.

L'Enfant's plan located public, private, and commercial buildings throughout the city to stimulate simultaneous development in all sections, but left much of the area open, available for improvement. He knew Washington would expand slowly over time; his design anticipated the "aggrandizement and embellishment" of the city as its financial resources allowed. Doubtless he did not anticipate how slow the expansion would be.

After making their way through the Maryland and Virginia forests, more than a few visitors were startled by the view that lay before them. The elegant city remained only a possibility; the broad avenues and grand buildings existed only on paper. A traveler reported back to his English relations:

> This country is far different from what we were
> taught to expect in England, and consequently I
> have been deceived in the expectations I formed
> on the descriptions which I had represented to
> me of this place.... The five streets so pompously
> lain out on the map which we examined in
> London, are avenues cut through the woods, with
> not a solitary house standing in either of them.

In 1796, three years after construction began on the Capitol and President's House, no private dwellings bordered the long street between them, and the city appeared as a "thick wood pierced with avenues." So undistinguished was the landscape that some travelers reportedly crossed the length of Washington without realizing where they were. Isaac Weld, an Englishman, was surprised to discover that, "Excepting the streets and avenues and a small part of the ground adjoining the public buildings, the whole place is covered with trees."

To many of the new country's citizens, more accustomed to thinking of themselves as Bostonians or Virginians than as Americans, the idea of building a national capital, let alone from the ground up, seemed highly unusual, and it caused serious political disruption. Between 1774 and 1783, the Continental Congress moved eight times in flight from British troops. The need for a secure and permanent seat of government was obvious, but its ideal location was not.

When Congress empowered President Washington to select the new capital's site on the Potomac River, it was after nearly a decade of extensive, often fierce debate. Northerners objected to building "palaces in the wilderness," and Thomas Jefferson wrote that the decision to locate the capital in the South "produced the most bitter and angry contests ever known in Congress, before or since the union of the States." Neither legislators nor the public accepted the location as final.

For the previous ten years, America's political affairs had been decided in Philadelphia, then the country's most cosmopolitan city. Philadelphians were so certain Congress would balk at the fearsome conditions along the Potomac and refuse to relocate that they erected a handsome home for the president in their city.

Deliberations continued, and many were surprised in the summer of 1800 when President Adams ordered the government's transfer to Washington. Through the summer and fall of 1800, the 131 employees of the Navy, Treasury, State, War, and Post Office Departments relocated to the new capital. In June small, curious crowds gathered as ships loaded with the nation's possessions arrived at the Potomac River wharves. From dockside the government's papers and furniture were unceremoniously carted to the two office buildings that flanked the unfinished President's House.

When it became clear in November 1800 that President Adams' decision was irrevocable, the country's political leaders left their Philadelphia lodgings for two long, cold days of travel over poorly marked, deeply rutted roads. Overnight accommodations at an inn somewhere in Maryland provided inelegant surroundings for the muddy travelers who sometimes had to share their beds with equally tired strangers. The stage departed for Washington around 3 or 4 A.M., and by the time it neared the city at dusk, the nation's lawmakers no doubt were ready for comfort and rest. But the first sight of their new

North wing of the Capitol. Birch, circa 1800.

home provided them with little hope of pleasure. "Our approach to the city was accompanied with sensations not easily described," wrote Connecticut Representative John Cotton Smith:

> One wing of the Capitol only had been erected, which, with the President's house, a mile distant from it, both constructed with white sandstone, were shining objects in dismal contrast with the scene around them. Instead of recognizing the avenues and streets portrayed on the plan of the city, not one was visible, unless we except a road with two buildings on each side of it, called the New Jersey avenue. The Pennsylvania [Avenue]... from the Capitol to the Presidential mansion was then nearly the whole distance a deep morass, covered with alder bushes.

John Adams preceded his wife Abigail to the city. His initial reaction to the scene could hardly have been more favorable than Smith's.

The President's House was encircled by carpenters' and masons' hovels, and Adams entered his new home by temporary stairs. Once inside he found only a few rooms habitable. There were no glass panes in the East Room windows and no stairs to the second floor. Perhaps choosing the best tack, he declined to describe the condition of the dwelling to his wife, explaining, "You will form the best idea of it from inspection."

Forced to cancel the opening session of Congress because a quorum could not be met, Adams greeted the 106 representatives and 32 senators of the Sixth Congress a few days later on November 21 in the Capitol's north wing. As noted by Congressman Smith, it was the building's only completed part and remained so for some time. Congress was so slow to assign money to the project that three years later the Capitol still appeared to an English visitor as "a ponderous unfinished mass of brick and stone."

Contemporary Washingtonians often complain about how expensive and difficult it is to find suitable lodging; apparently this problem plagued the city's earliest residents as well. When he arrived in June 1800 to open the Post Office Department, Assistant Postmaster General Abraham Bradley reported to his family, "It is impossible that all the people attached to the public offices should be accommodated with houses, the few that have been left are at [yearly] rents none under $250 and $300." Some government officials moved to Georgetown, and many more found lodging in boarding houses near the Capitol that offered spare but affordable accommodations.

West of the Capitol, along what is now the Mall, L'Enfant set aside an area for the "spacious houses and gardens" of foreign diplomatic corps, but few countries sent representatives. Three years before the government moved to Washington, District of Columbia commissioners contacted a number of foreign governments to offer embassy sites. Only the Portuguese minister responded. Officials eagerly granted a deed for land to the Queen of Portugal, but no residence was erected. By 1803, four diplomats lived in the city. Legal difficulties hampered the construction of embassies, and the few foreign representatives assigned to the new nation rented quarters in Georgetown or joined American officials in hotels and boarding houses. Much later Embassy Row was pieced together in the city's West End, far from L'Enfant's site.

Familiar with the sophisticated comforts of Philadelphia, where men and women moved through paved streets in fashionable dress, and theaters and concert halls offered public entertainment almost every night, Washington's residents found conditions in the new capital especially objectionable. During the summer months everyone who could find a carriage left to escape the heat. The exasperation of many was voiced by the French diplomat who exclaimed, "My God, what have I done to be condemned to reside in such a city!"

For Abigail Adams the most difficult part of the move was finding the city; she and her party spent several hours of their journey to Washington lost in the forests of Maryland. Upon reaching her destination, however, she wrote that the city was "a beautiful spot, capable of any improvements, and the more I view it the more I am delighted with it." Congressman Smith admitted, "Notwithstanding the unfavorable aspect which Washington presented on our arrival, I cannot sufficiently express my admiration of its local position," and he thought the views from the city constituted a "prospect of surpassing beauty and grandeur."

Most who came to Washington adjusted to their situation, and gradually a society composed of the capital's permanent residents and the never-ending stream of newcomers took shape.

Capitol after conflagration. Strickland, 1814.

The War of 1812 dealt a serious blow to the city's development. Washington's status at the time was still so insignificant that few expected the British fleet to attack the capital when they could concentrate their forces on ports along the Atlantic. Thus, the city was virtually undefended on August 24, 1814, when British Admiral George Cockburn marched his troops onto the Capitol grounds.

Twenty-four hours later, they left Washington in smoldering ruins.

Destruction of the nation's capital reopened the debate on its location. Margaret Bayard Smith, who chronicled the city's early history, wrote, "I do not suppose the Government will ever return to Washington. All those whose property was invested in that place will be reduced to poverty."

Fortunately Smith was wrong, and Washington settled into its role as the permanent seat of national government. The architect Benjamin Henry Latrobe, a keen observer of the city's social and political scene, penned shortly after the close of the war, "A greater benefit could not have accrued to this city than the destruction of its principal buildings by the British." He, of course, benefitted handsomely from commissions that came his way in rebuilding Washington. Local bankers and leading citizens raised a temporary capitol on the site where the Supreme Court building now stands and extended $500,000 in loans to reconstruct the city. Thomas Jefferson offered his private library to replace the Congressional library burned by the British in 1814, the Madisons returned to

the rebuilt White House in 1817, Congress reoccupied the Capitol in 1819, and shops and houses began to cluster around the newly erected public buildings.

St. John's Church. Benjamin Henry Latrobe, circa 1820.

One of the most striking changes in postwar Washington was the formation of affluent neighborhoods. The one which grew up around Lafayette Square, directly across from the President's House in an area L'Enfant had designated as the President's Park, soon became the center of Washington's political and social life.

St. John's Church, which stands at the corner of 16th and H Streets on Lafayette Square, was the neighborhood's first significant building. Latrobe's original design, now altered by the addition of a portico and tower, owed much to the Neoclassical style then popular in France.

Shortly after its completion, the architect boasted to his son, "I have just completed a church that made many Washingtonians religious who had not been religious before."

The widely admired building enhanced the demand for Latrobe's services. Commissions for several important houses boosted his reputation, and in 1818, he was hired to build Lafayette Square's first private dwelling. His client, Commodore Stephen Decatur, had sailed to the North African coast where his celebrated battles with the Barbary pirates ended years of plunder and extortion of American vessels and made him a wealthy man. Later he earned a reputation as a hero in clashes with the British navy during the War of 1812. The naval officer lived here just over a year before he was killed in a duel. Henry Clay and Vice President Martin Van Buren later occupied the house, which still stands at the southwest corner of Jackson Place and H Street.

Latrobe's design set the scale and style for the Blair House, the building that today forms the nucleus of the President's Guest House. It was the next private dwelling erected in the Lafayette Square neighborhood. Dr. Joseph Lovell, an accomplished physician from Boston, was the original owner of the house. Educated at Harvard College and Harvard Medical School, Lovell earned the respect of Army officials as a surgeon in the War of 1812. When he was named the first surgeon general of the Army in 1818, Lovell moved to Washington. Like most newcomers, he probably lived in a boarding house or rented temporary quarters until he purchased the residence across from the President's House. Lovell took possession in time for the festivities that surrounded the 1824 visit of the Marquis de Lafayette, including the renaming of the nearby park in his honor.

The architect or builder of Lovell's house is unknown, suggesting that no one of Latrobe's stature was responsible for its design. Most likely it was constructed by a local builder who adapted its plan and details from one of the period's many popular architectural pattern books. Although the house has been raised from its original two stories and remodeled to suit changing architectural tastes, its basic form and some of its original trim remain intact. At the time Joseph Lovell was directing the construction of his brick dwelling, most Washingtonians lived in modest frame structures. But while Dr. Lovell's Classical Revival-style residence must have appeared palatial to many, it was far less elaborate than the nearby Octagon and Decatur Houses.

With eleven children and a high public profile, the Lovells required ample living and entertaining quarters, and these needs were neatly accommodated by the arrangement of the house's interior spaces. Typical of the period, its four-room plan reveals clues about the domestic routines and social activities of those who lived there.

Decatur House.
E. Vaile, 1822.

Lovell probably greeted visitors in the center passage, where modern guests are welcomed, and ushered them into the appropriate adjacent room. Much of the house's first floor was divided into several dining and drawing rooms. These names, however, denote only their primary function, for the spaces routinely served multiple purposes. Family friend Juliana Gales Seaton described just such a situation when she recalled the ball she and her husband, owner of Washington's first newspaper, the *National Intelligencer,* gave at the Seaton home for the Marquis de Lafayette in December 1824. "My chamber and the large nursery were *deranged* and *arranged* for the occasion, serving as card and supper rooms. We danced in the dining and drawing rooms."

The smallest of all the first-story chambers, now known as the Lincoln Room, may have been used for both intimate gatherings and important functions. It later served as an office. The two large drawing rooms on the other side of the center passage could be arranged for public occasions. Formal dinners as well as some family meals were probably held in one of the first-story chambers. During especially lavish or large events, the rooms on this floor could be opened to provide a circuit of entertaining spaces similar to those described by Juliana Seaton.

Lovell and his wife were very much a part of Washington's increasingly active society. Evening events were sometimes just a brief walk from their home, as some of the city's finest hosts lived in the brick townhouses bordering Lafayette Square. At various times Henry Clay, Daniel Webster, Martin Van Buren, and a number of other 19th-century political leaders lived in the neighborhood. After her husband's death, Dolley Madison moved to the square's east side. Early in this century, famed historian and social critic Henry Adams, himself a resident, remarked, "La Fayette Square was society."

From December to May when Congress was in session, calendars filled quickly with parties, balls, and dinners, the style of which changed with each new administration. John Adams, the first president to live in Washington, attempted to recreate Philadelphia's social life by adopting the formality that marked George Washington's presidency. When Thomas Jefferson occupied the President's House, he replaced formal balls with public receptions and favored small, intimate suppers known for stimulating conversation. Guests at Jefferson's late afternoon dinners included American politicians and foreign diplomats as well as, on an occasion or two, an Indian chief and his entourage. From 1809 to 1829, the administrations of James Madison, James Monroe, and John Quincy Adams revived the practice of hosting more formal official gatherings.

An ever-growing diplomatic corps was welcomed into the social fabric of the capital city, and its presence increased the number of receptions, dinners, and balls. While most events were held in private homes, the city's fashionable also gathered in newly built public assembly rooms for evenings of cards, dancing, gossip, and a bit of official business.

When Andrew Jackson was inaugurated in the spring of 1829, Washington's social and political tone changed. The first president from the West, he was also the first without ties to New England and politically influential Virginia. As hero of the Battle of New Orleans, Jackson had an enormous appeal to the common voter. Fittingly he was the first president to be sworn in publicly on the Capitol steps. After Chief Justice John Marshall administered the oath of office, Jackson rode to the President's House to preside at a reception open to all who wanted to shake his hand. Thousands of well-wishers preceded him down Pennsylvania Avenue, and Jackson arrived to a mob scene. The excited crowd swept through the house, leaving broken china and furniture in

their wake. Jackson quickly retreated to a boarding house, where he spent his first night as president. Refreshments were carried to the White House lawn in "tubs and buckets," and the party continued for hours without the guest of honor. So disastrous was the evening that such open and undignified receptions were never held again.

Andrew Jackson's inaugural reception. Robert Cruikshank, 1829.

However, in general, official events during Jackson's term in office were less formal than in previous administrations.

From the first days of the Jackson administration, a bitter, divisive struggle raged between Secretary of State Martin Van Buren and Vice President John C. Calhoun. Relying little on advice from his embattled cabinet, Jackson preferred to confer with the small group of men critics called his "Kitchen Cabinet." It quickly became evident that of these advisers, most of whom came from Kentucky and Tennessee, journalist Francis Preston Blair held the most sway with the president.

The enduring friendship between Jackson and Blair had an unpromising beginning. During Blair's move from Kentucky in 1830, his family's carriage overturned just a few miles out of Washington. Blair suffered a serious cut on his head that was closed by stitches and covered with a rather unattractive, large plaster patch. As soon as the family reached Washington, Jackson's aides, anxious for the two to meet, ushered the wrinkled, battered Blair to dinner at the White House. The unassuming editor and the president got along famously. Little known when he arrived in Washington, Blair's name became synonymous with national politics for much of the 19th century.

Francis Preston Blair initially caught the attention of the president's friends and advisers because of the pro-Jackson articles he penned for the *Argus of Western America,* a newspaper published in Frankfort, Kentucky. Needing a strong partisan voice, Jackson offered Blair an opportunity to shape political thought as editor of Washington's pro-administration newspaper, the *Globe.*

Francis Preston Blair was 40 when he and his wife Eliza decided to move to the capital city. Under his quick pen, the paper prospered. Five years after it commenced publication, 17,000 subscribers received the *Globe.* Articles reprinted in other papers extended its influence. A portion of its wide circulation was due to the fact that party members were forced to subscribe. But Blair's fine writing and the *Globe's* news features, advice literature, and book reviews added to its appeal. Eliza Blair was an active partner in her husband's publishing business. She prepared articles on the arts, wrote reviews, covered the "ladies' news," and was an early advocate for the economic and professional rights of women.

Finding adequate and affordable housing proved as difficult for the Blairs as it had for other new arrivals, and they occupied a succession of rented lodgings until 1836. That year an advertisement announced the availability of the Lovell House, "a spacious two story brick building, with a basement...a well of

Cover of the Globe, *August 16, 1836.*

excellent water in the yard; brick stable and carriage house adjoining the alley; flower and fruit garden tastefully laid out and highly cultivated." The Decatur House was also on the market, and Blair briefly contemplated buying it. Warned by Vice President Van Buren that some might consider showy behavior unfitting a man of his political beliefs, Blair purchased the less elaborate Lovell House for $6,500, just as Jackson was about to leave office.

The move placed the family in the midst of Lafayette Square society, which they both enjoyed despite Francis Preston Blair's difficult introduction to the peculiarities of the capital's social customs. Asked to an evening's gathering at seven o'clock, he came at the appointed hour. No one had warned him that Washington guests timed their arrival according to their rank. At this particular party, members of Congress arrived at nine; an hour later cabinet members appeared; and at eleven the president and his guest were greeted. Despite the gaffe, Blair reported the night as one to remember:

> I behaved very well among the canvas-back
> ducks, the turkeys without bones, the oysters and
> the quail...I drank Rhenish and Flemish sherry
> and champagne...I tried chocolate custards and
> jellies of all sorts, and a variety of things I could
> not find out after trying them...I came home this
> morning with a sad headache.

In conclusion he joked, "I must give up the *Globe* or the beau monde."

The Blairs never entered fully into "the beau monde," concentrating instead on their business interests and family affairs. With his partner John C. Rives, Blair established the *Congressional Globe,* a daily report of Congressional proceedings which became the *Congressional Record* in 1873. Throughout the Van Buren administration, the *Globe* spoke for the Democratic party, and Blair moved easily across the House and Senate floors, gathering stories. So effective were his withering editorials against the opposition that it is said he ruined many careers. With Van Buren's defeat in 1840, the paper's influence diminished, but Blair continued as editor for five more years. His increasingly independent editorials began to anger some Democratic leaders who believed— correctly so—that he could no longer be counted on to promote the party line. In 1845, newly elected President James Polk forced him out of the publishing business, which Blair sold for a profit.

Three years before, the Blairs had purchased land northwest of the city and built a house there called Silver Spring, from which the present Maryland suburb takes its name. After Francis Preston Blair's removal from the *Globe,* his family moved to Silver Spring, returning to Washington only for brief visits.

Blair's decision to leave the city enabled him to realize his long-standing ambition to live as a gentleman farmer. He may also have been responding both to the growing body of literature describing the benefits of life in the country and to the still-rough conditions that prevailed in much of the capital. "This is how it is in Washington—streets not paved, swept or lighted," observed one French visitor in 1840:

> My carriage sank up to the axle-tree in the snow
> and mud.... The nights are so noisy that one can
> scarcely sleep. There is a continual uproar, the
> reason for which is that the inhabitants all own
> cows and pigs, but no stables, and these animals
> wander about all day and all night through the
> city.... The nocturnal wanderings of these beasts
> create an infernal racket, in which they are joined
> by dogs and cats.

Flight to the country may indeed have provided a welcomed relief.

During the Blairs' absence, the Blair House continued to be the scene of political action. Several important national figures attracted by the dwelling's location leased it from 1845 until 1852. Its first tenant was George Bancroft, secretary of the Navy; during his brief stay, he established the U.S. Naval Academy at Annapolis. John Y. Mason took over both Bancroft's position and his residence in 1846. Three years later, Secretary of the Interior Thomas Ewing moved his family to the Blair House for a short period. Ewing's daughter Ellen married the young soldier William Tecumseh Sherman in a gala wedding, one of twelve held at the house. Sherman later distinguished himself as a Union general in the Civil War. Thomas Corwin, secretary of the Treasury, was the last tenant before the Blairs once again took possession.

While the romance and seemingly limitless possibilities of the western frontier had attracted all three Blair sons, two also developed a taste for political life. The eldest, Montgomery, took up residence at the Blair House when he returned to Washington from Missouri in 1854 to practice law. Drawn to politics, he later served as postmaster general during Abraham Lincoln's administration. Among his accomplishments as head of the Post Office Department was the introduction of free mail delivery. Letters and packages had been delivered in the country's urban areas since the early 1800s, but recipients were required to

pay the mail carrier a penny or two for each delivered item. Keeping mail service flowing during the Civil War was no easy task, and Blair devised a number of effective means to do so.

It was during Montgomery Blair's occupancy that the house, in 1866, was raised to four stories and its exterior walls stuccoed and scored to resemble stone. Blair kept his wife Mary apprised of the construction during her absence. "Your house has at last reached its full height and it is a pretty great one," he proudly informed her. The work caught the attention of acquaintances who inquired how high Blair intended to go. He reported to Mary his reply, "I am getting up in the world you see," and when it was finished, he boasted, "The house is magnificent in appearance and every body agrees that it is now the finest and most complete of any in the city."

Portrait of Montgomery Blair. Casimir Gregory Stapko after Thomas Sully, 1968.

Until 1859, the Blair House stood alone in its block northwest of the White House. In that year, Francis Preston Blair built the house at what is now 1623 Pennsylvania Avenue for his daughter, Elizabeth "Lizzie" Blair Lee, and her husband, Admiral Samuel Phillips Lee. Lee was a member of the famous Virginia family which included Richard Henry Lee, Francis Lightfoot Lee, and Robert E. Lee. Phillips Lee, a career naval officer, spent much of the early period of his marriage at sea, while Elizabeth remained with her parents at Silver Spring. Lee's first efforts at securing a separate residence in the area met with strenuous objections, both from his wife and her family. Elizabeth explained her resistance, writing her husband, "You are a wanderer and will necessarily leave me utterly desolate in your absence." Construction of the Lee House adjacent to the Blair House, where Elizabeth had spent much of her youth, may have represented something of a compromise between the two competing interests. Francis and Eliza Blair also apparently needed a place to stay when they came into the city. Relations with Montgomery and his wife had soured after a quarrel between Eliza and her daughter-in-law, and the Francis Preston Blairs no longer felt comfortable in their former home.

The Lincoln administration was the last with which the Blairs were closely identified; after Abraham Lincoln's death, while the Blairs continued to be politically active, their influence diminished. Montgomery Blair's second son, Gist Blair, like his father, returned to Washington early in this century from Missouri where he had practiced law. He was the last Blair to live in the house, occupying it until his death in 1940.

During the Second World War, the United States' involvement in international affairs increased dramatically. President Franklin D. Roosevelt's famous radio addresses were broadcast around the world, and an unprecedented number of official visitors and heads of state traveled to confer with the dynamic leader in the Oval Office. At the time, it was customary for the president's guests to spend the first night of their visit in the White House and move the following day to a hotel, embassy, or house in the city.

Blair-Lee House, April 23, 1945.

Although Washington's hotels filled to overflowing with foreign representatives, a frugal Congress remained unconvinced of the need for an official guest house and repeatedly rejected State Department requests for assistance.

Years later, the president's son, Franklin, Jr., recalled that it was probably Winston Churchill who finally provoked the government to act on its need to suitably house visiting chiefs of state and heads of government. According to Franklin, Jr., early one morning near the family's private quarters, his mother found Churchill wandering down the corridor still in his nightshirt, his trademark cigar in his hand.

"What are you doing here, Mr. Prime Minister?" Eleanor Roosevelt inquired.

"I've come down to have breakfast with your husband."

"You kept him up until 3 A.M. this morning, Mr. Prime Minister. He isn't up yet." And she directed her distinguished guest back to his bedroom.

Probably not too long after this encounter, Stanley Woodward, President Roosevelt's chief of protocol, arranged to purchase the Blair House as the nation's guest house. President Manuel Prado of Peru was the first Blair House guest in May 1942. Representatives of the Soviet Union, Greece, New Zealand, Colombia, Ecuador, Cuba, Venezuela, Poland, and Yugoslavia followed in quick succession later that year.

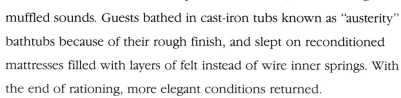

In 1943, when the number of visiting dignitaries exceeded the number of available Blair House rooms, the State Department acquired as an annex the Lee House, which had long been used as an office building. Both houses were renovated during the war, but their privileged status did not exempt them from rationing. According to contemporary newspaper accounts, the Blair House staff searched antique stores for secondhand pieces to complete silver services because of the ban on silverware production. Wool carpeting was impossible to obtain, so cotton rugs muffled sounds. Guests bathed in cast-iron tubs known as "austerity" bathtubs because of their rough finish, and slept on reconditioned mattresses filled with layers of felt instead of wire inner springs. With the end of rationing, more elegant conditions returned.

Harry S. Truman at the Blair House, November 21, 1948.

When serious structural problems forced extensive rebuilding at the White House, the Blair House became a private home once again, occupied by President Truman and his family from 1948 to 1952. Few changes were necessary to accommodate its new function as temporary presidential quarters, and the Trumans settled comfortably into the

house just as their guests had done before them. The image of President Truman leaving the Blair House each morning for the quick walk across Pennsylvania Avenue to his White House became familiar to Americans.

Dwight D. Eisenhower and King Saud of Saudi Arabia at the Blair House, January 30, 1957.

In 1955, during President Dwight D. Eisenhower's administration, the tradition of spending the first night in the White House ended, and guests were driven from National Airport or their train at Union Station directly to the Blair House. When the number of state visits decreased after the war, the arrival of official guests became occasions for festive, open-convertible parades, and flag-waving schoolchildren lined the route to greet celebrated visitors. In 1957, to underscore its important function, the Blair House was officially designated the President's Guest House.

Extensive refurbishing during the administrations of John F. Kennedy and Lyndon B. Johnson provided a much-needed renewal and sustained the house during the next two decades of heavy use. In 1982, Blair House officials decided once again to close the house to overnight visitors—this time for the most extensive repairs and remodeling to date.

The transition of the Blair House from private home to the President's Guest House was nearly a seamless one. When the State Department purchased the dwelling in 1942, it acquired the Blair family's furniture, china, and silver as well. Although the house was partially redecorated, no substantial changes were made to prepare it for its new role. One day it was the home of a prominent American family, and the next day it opened its doors as the nation's guest house.

While today it takes four houses and a new wing unified under the Blair House name to accomplish the complex task of playing host to guests of the president of the United States, the staff works hard to preserve the intimate, familial atmosphere established by the Blair family housekeeper and first Blair House manager, Victoria Geaney.

Their efforts do not pass unnoticed. A recent visitor paid tribute to their warm attentiveness when he signed the Blair House Guest Book, "In deep gratitude…we felt like we were at home."

The Blair House is an important component of America's official hospitality. Beyond the quiet, dignified parlors and dining rooms, a network of meeting rooms, offices, and switchboards ensures the smooth operation of a guest's government continents away.

*Blair Front
Drawing Room, 1945.*

But more than this, the Blair House is a secluded retreat from the conference table and official events, where the nation's guests can relax as if in their own home. Apparently the Blair House succeeds wonderfully in this task. Kings and queens have kicked off their shoes and invited their friends over for late night gatherings, chiefs of state have romped through the house with laughing grandchildren on their backs, and more than one visiting young dignitary has enjoyed a birthday party in the dining room.

Francis and Eliza Blair would find this continued gracious use of their home altogether fitting. From its furnishings to its color schemes, from its evening meals to its cordial staff, the Blair House accurately reflects an ever-evolving American culture and represents the hospitality this country would offer to the world.

In its commitment to harmonious relations among all peoples, the United States of America hopes that the good will which underlies global peace and understanding may begin, in part, at the Blair House.

Blair Front Drawing Room; *(overleaf)* Blair House Entrance Hall   31

In the spring of 1861, three days after the attack on Fort Sumter, South Carolina, signaled the beginning of the Civil War, Francis Preston Blair greeted Colonel Robert E. Lee in what is now known as the Lincoln Room. Abraham Lincoln wanted to discover whether the highly respected officer might lead the Union army, but did not wish to call Lee to his office. Instead, he sought the assistance of his friend Francis Preston Blair, whose daughter had married one of Lee's cousins. After thoughtful consideration, Lee declined, asking, "How can I draw my sword upon Virginia, my native State?" Soon after, he accepted command of the Confederate Army of Northern Virginia.

When the Blair House ceased to be a private residence and welcomed its first official guests in 1942, those guests saw a house much as the Blairs knew it, filled with the family's 19th-century furniture, linen, Aubusson carpets, and Chinese export porcelain. A tankard crafted by the American silversmith and patriot Paul Revere was among the prized possessions acquired by the State Department.

Like any other old dwelling, the Blair House has needed and received repeated repairs, painting, and plastering through the years. State Department officials were planning to update the house with fresh paint, new upholstery, and modern appliances when a loose chandelier threatened to fall on a guest room bed in 1982, and the project quickly expanded to include extensive structural repairs as well. Architects, engineers, and workmen worked for almost six years to completely refurbish the houses that comprise the President's Guest House. The addition of a new wing at the rear of the original structure dramatically enlarged the Blair House. Internationally known interior decorators Mario Buatta and Mark Hampton added new upholstery, chandeliers, Oriental rugs, and lavishly ornate curtains to unify the four houses into a beautiful single composition. The renovation, the most extensive ever executed at the Blair House, was completed during the administration of Ronald Reagan.

The original interior details at the Blair House were simple, reflecting the architectural tastes of the 1820s. Gist Blair installed a good deal of the interior trim, including the distinctive plasterwork, door surrounds, chair rails, and cornices, after he took possession of the property in 1910. Blair, who grew up in the house, probably decided to bring the parlors, dining room, and library up to the decorative standards of public rooms in the city's other important private residences.

ompleted in 1988, the two-story Garden Wing is almost as large as the original Blair House. It is built of sandstone from Ohio, similar in color and quality to the exterior masonry of the White House, which was quarried in the 1790s from George Washington's land along the Potomac River.

Receptions, dinners, and parties formerly were confined to the small 19th-century dining rooms in the Blair and Lee Houses. The Garden Room addition provides a stunning setting for large official gatherings.

Just beyond the Garden Room, the newly landscaped terrace offers a serene retreat amid native plant materials, antique garden furniture, and a Victorian fountain from the collection of the Smithsonian Institution.

*P*lans for the care and comfort of distinguished visitors begin months before they
arrive in Washington. Hard work and meticulous
preparations allow the Blair House to function
smoothly as both home and office to monarchs,
chiefs of state, and heads of government conduct-
ing their business in Washington, where state
visits most often mean a constant round of
meetings, press conferences, and gala dinners.
While many of these functions are held in the
house, it also offers three full floors of quiet
bedrooms and sitting rooms where visitors can
relax in privacy.

45

(Above) Jackson Place Dining Room

46   (Right) Jackson Place Sitting Room

W̶hat is known as the Blair House is actually four different houses joined to form one residence with more than 100 rooms. The centerpiece of the complex is the original Blair House, home to three generations of the politically influential Blair family. The Lee House, next door at 1653 Pennsylvania Avenue, was built for Francis Preston Blair's daughter, who married Robert E. Lee's cousin. Two Victorian-era row houses facing Lafayette Square complete the ensemble.

The management of the house is directed from basement-level offices. Beautifully furnished first-floor parlors and dining rooms serve as backdrops for state events and elegant evenings, just as they did when the Blair family occupied the house. In private quarters on the upper floors, guests, their families, and aides rest between official duties.

Portrait of Francis Preston Blair by Thomas Sully, 1845.

rom 1948 to 1952, the Blair House was known as the Truman White House. When a leg of the Truman family piano broke through the White House floor, the building's central portion was closed for its most extensive structural work since the 19th century, and the president, his wife, and daughter moved across the street.

Few special accommodations were made to outfit the house in its new role as the temporary White House. Harry Truman, who loved his walk around the Lafayette Park neighborhood on his way to the Oval Office, often posed under the Blair House portico for reporters before setting out. He chose a front parlor of the Lee House, with its view of Pennsylvania Avenue and the Old Executive Office Building, as his study.

*H*istorically, United States presidents have moved with ease between the White House and the Blair House. Francis Preston Blair was the most influential member of Andrew Jackson's informal "Kitchen Cabinet," and the two often conferred. Martin Van Buren valued Blair's advice, as did Abraham Lincoln 20 years later. Lincoln also appointed Montgomery Blair postmaster general in his first administration. Harry Truman, who called Blair House home for much of his second term, made the quick trip between the house and the Oval Office several times each day. John Kennedy sometimes extended diplomatic meetings informally by walking his guests back to the Blair House.

A ll diplomatic visits and Blair House operations are coordinated by the Department of State. Thomas Jefferson, appointed first secretary of state by George Washington in 1789, directed the newly independent country's foreign affairs with five assistants and twelve overseas ministers. Some 70 years later, the department had grown to a total of only 31 staff members. Like all other government agencies, the Department of State expanded tremendously during World War II, and today numbers more than 14,000.

Until 1947, the Department of State was headquartered in the magnificent French Renaissance-style structure now known as the Old Executive Office Building next to the White House and just across from the Blair House. The secretary of state and chief of protocol could simply stroll across Pennsylvania Avenue to meet dignitaries at the Blair House without having to arrange for limousines and motorcades.

M *any guests get their first glimpse of life in the United States during their stay at the*
Blair House. The residence contains both English and American antiques, many of
which are pieces from the Blair family collection. American food is the specialty of the house.
Second-floor library shelves feature American literature. And just beyond the Blair House
portico lies the city of Washington, where monument after magnificent monument recalls the
nation's past.

*legance is the hallmark of the Primary Suite,
where the nation's highest-ranking guests stay
during their Washington visit. Previously, chiefs of state
and heads of government stayed in a smaller suite on the
second floor of the original Blair House. Now, the entire
second level of the new wing is dedicated to the principal
guest quarters. Mahogany doors open into the three-room
Primary Suite appointed with priceless 18th-century
English antiques and fine paintings, all a gift of the
Heathcote Art Foundation. Moiré coverings, high ceilings,
and deeply molded plaster cornices impart an air of
subdued formality to the rooms.

BLAIR HOUSE RESTORATION OF 1982-1988

BLAIR HOUSE PROJECT CHAIRMAN

Selwa Roosevelt
Chief of Protocol

INTERIOR DECORATORS

Mario Buatta and Mark Hampton

ARCHITECTS

John I Mesick and John G. Waite

LANDSCAPE ARCHITECTS

Richard K. Webel and Richard C. Webel

CURATOR

Clement E. Conger

MURALIST

Robert Jackson

**ARCHITECTURAL CONSULTANT
TO THE DECORATORS**

Allan Greenberg

**OFFICERS OF THE BLAIR HOUSE
RESTORATION FUND**

The Honorable Selwa Roosevelt
Chief of Protocol
Honorary Chairman

The Honorable Anne Armstrong
President

Robin Chandler Duke
Vice President

Carol Laxalt
Secretary

John W. Hanes, Jr.
Treasurer

David Jacobson
Counsel to the Fund

DIRECTORS

Mr. John W. Hanes, Jr.
Mrs. Paul Laxalt
Mrs. Merle Thorpe, Jr.
Mrs. Maurice B. Tobin
Mrs. Eric Weinmann

EXECUTIVE DIRECTORS

Mrs. Patricia A. Bye
1987-1988
Mrs. Carter Cunningham
1988

WASHINGTON COMMITTEE

Mrs. Robert H. Charles
Mrs. Charles Z. Wick

LONDON COMMITTEE

Fleur Cowles

GARDEN COMMITTEE

Mrs. Eric Weinmann

**NATIONAL COUNCIL FOR THE
BLAIR HOUSE RESTORATION FUND**

Mr. Joe L. Allbritton
Washington, D.C.

Mrs. James Alsdorf
Winnetka, Illinois

Mr. Dwayne O. Andreas
Decatur, Illinois

The Honorable Leonore Annenberg
Wynnewood, Pennsylvania

The Honorable Walter H. Annenberg
Wynnewood, Pennsylvania

Mrs. Vincent Astor
New York, New York

The Honorable Winton Blount
Montgomery, Alabama

Mrs. John de Braganca
Winston-Salem, North Carolina

Mrs. Willard C. Butcher
Wilton, Connecticut

The Honorable Anne Cox Chambers
Atlanta, Georgia

Mrs. Robert H. Charles
Washington, D.C.

The Honorable Holland H. Coors
Denver, Colorado

The Honorable C. Douglas Dillon
and Mrs. Dillon
New York, New York

Mrs. Brooke H. Duncan II
New Orleans, Louisiana

Mr. Christopher Forbes
Far Hills, New Jersey

Mrs. Gordon P. Getty
San Francisco, California

Mrs. Katharine Meyer Graham
Washington, D.C.

Mrs. Henry L. Hillman
Pittsburgh, Pennsylvania

Mrs. James Stewart Hooker
New York, New York

Mrs. Michael Huffington
Houston, Texas

Mr. John H. Johnson
Chicago, Illinois

Mr. Donald Kendall
Purchase, New York

Mrs. Lane Kirkland
Washington, D.C.

Mrs. Joseph H. Lauder
New York, New York

Mrs. Jean C. Lindsey
Laurel, Mississippi

Mrs. Eugene McDermott
Dallas, Texas

Mr. Barnabas McHenry
New York, New York

Mrs. Jack C. Massey
Nashville, Tennessee

Mr. David H. Murdock
Los Angeles, California

Mrs. H. Ross Perot
Dallas, Texas

Mrs. Annette Reed
New York, New York

Mrs. James D. Robinson III
New York, New York

Mr. David Rockefeller
New York, New York

Mr. and Mrs. Arthur Ross
New York, New York

Mrs. B. Francis Saul II
Chevy Chase, Maryland

Mr. Liener Temerlin
Dallas, Texas

Mr. Jerry Weintraub
Beverly Hills, California

Mrs. Keith S. Wellin
New York, New York

Mrs. Charles Z. Wick
Washington, D.C.

Mr. Walter B. Wriston
New York, New York

Mr. Mortimer B. Zuckerman
New York, New York

BENEFACTORS

(Gifts of $100,000 or more)

Mr. and Mrs. Joe L. Allbritton
Mr. and Mrs. Dwayne O. Andreas
Mr. and Mrs. Walter H. Annenberg
Mr. and Mrs. Robert Bass
Mr. and Mrs. Winton Blount
Mrs. Anne Cox Chambers
Mr. and Mrs. C. Douglas Dillon
Ann and Gordon Getty
Mr. and Mrs. Henry L. Hillman
Mrs. James Stewart Hooker
Mr. and Mrs. Michael Jaharis, Jr.
Mr. and Mrs. John H. Johnson
Mr. and Mrs. Jack Carroll Massey
Mr. David Murdock
Mr. and Mrs. Gerald Oppenheimer
Mr. and Mrs. H. Ross Perot
Mrs. Annette Reed
Mr. and Mrs. David Rockefeller
Mr. and Mrs. Arthur Ross
Mr. Lewis Rudin
Mr. and Mrs. B. Francis Saul II
Mr. and Mrs. Jerry Weintraub
Mrs. Keith S. Wellin
Mr. John C. Whitehead
Mr. Mortimer B. Zuckerman

FOUNDATIONS

The Adolph Coors Foundation
The Armand Hammer Foundation
The Eugene McDermott Foundation
Heathcote Art Foundation, Incorporated
Jules and Doris Stein Foundation
The Vincent Astor Foundation

CORPORATE BENEFACTORS

American Express Company
American Standard, Inc.
Bloomingdale's
Chase Manhattan Bank, N.A.
Elizabeth Arden
Ford Motor Company
General Electric Company
Hobart Corporation
Lenox
Occidental Petroleum Company
PepsiCo, Inc.
Sears, Roebuck and Co.
Tiffany & Co.
The Washington Post Company

COMPANIES REPRODUCING THE STATELY HOMES OF THE BRITISH ISLES COLLECTIONS SELECTED BY SIR HUMPHREY WAKEFIELD, BT.

The Baker Furniture Company
Fieldcrest-Cannon, Inc.
Karastan Rugs
Mirror Fair
Mottahedeh
Stroheim & Romann
Tiffany & Co.

BLAIR HOUSE GARDENS PRINCIPAL DONORS

Mr. and Mrs. Arthur Ross
The Arthur and Janet Ross Garden
Fleur Cowles
The Courtyard Garden
Mr. and Mrs. Jack C. Massey
The Front Gardens

BLAIR HOUSE MAJOR DONORS
(Gifts of $10,000-$100,000)

Mr. and Mrs. Tobin Armstrong
Mr. and Mrs. William N. Cafritz
Mrs. Robert H. Charles
Mr. and Mrs. John B. Coleman
Mr. Max M. Fisher
Forbes Foundation
Mr. Henry Ford II
Mr. and Mrs. John W. Hanes, Jr.
Mr. and Mrs. Henry J. Heinz II
Mrs. Joseph H. Lauder
Mrs. Jean C. Lindsey
Mr. and Mrs. Robert L. McNeil, Jr.
Mr. Wayne Newton
Mr. and Mrs. Mandell Ourisman
Mr. Alexander P. Papamarkou
Mr. and Mrs. Frederick H. Prince IV
Mr. and Mrs. Donald T. Regan
Mr. and Mrs. James Regan
Mr. and Mrs. Archibald Roosevelt
Mr. and Mrs. Raymond Sagov
Dr. A. Jess Shenson
Dr. Ben Shenson
The Secretary of State
and Mrs. George P. Shultz
Mr. Bruce G. Sundlun
Mr. and Mrs. A. Alfred Taubman
Mr. and Mrs. Maurice Tobin

MAJOR DONORS FOUNDATIONS AND COMPANIES

AMR/American Airlines Foundation
American Federation of Labor
and Congress of Industrial Organizations
The Boeing Company
Bozell, Jacobs, Kenyon
& Eckhardt, Inc. Foundation
D. Swarvoski & Co.
Doris Leslie Blau, Inc.
Gates Foundation
High Winds Fund, Inc.
James G. Hanes Memorial Fund/Foundation
Mason & Hamlin/Sohmer Piano Company
Reid & Priest
The Riggs National Bank
of Washington, D.C.
Rosecore Carpet Company
BDO/Seidman
Simmons, U.S.A.
Stainless Fabricating Company
Stark Carpet Corporation
Washington Gas
Waterford Wedgwood

MAJOR DONORS—GIFTS-IN-KIND

FABRIC HOUSES
Brunschwig & Fils, Inc.
Clarence House
Cowtan & Tout
Fonthill, Ltd.
Fortuny, Inc.
Lee Jofa, Inc.
Quadrille
Scalamandre

TEXTILE COMPANIES
Chatham Manufacturing Company
Fieldcrest-Cannon, Inc.
J. P. Stevens & Company, Inc.
Laura Ashley, Inc.
Milliken & Company
Wamsutta/Pacific

RETAIL ESTABLISHMENTS
Garfinckel's
Hammacher Schlemmer
Hechinger's
The Horchow Collection
Lord and Taylor
Neiman-Marcus
Woodward and Lothrop

BLAIR HOUSE GARDEN CONTRIBUTORS TO THE DAVID CAMPBELL MEMORIAL FUND

American Society of Landscape Architects
in memory of member David Campbell
Mr. John Aniello
Stuart and Wilma Bernstein
Mr. William McCormick Blair, Jr.
Mr. Jeffery R. Carson
Mr. Antony Childs
Suzanne H. Donaldson
Mr. Daniel B. Flournoy, Jr.
Dr. and Mrs. Joe B. Goldberg
Dr. and Mrs. George Z. Heimbach
Mr. William B. Hoover, Jr.
Mr. H. Blount Hunter III
Mr. James M. Kline
Mr. C. S. Luck
Ellen T. McDougall
Mr. Paul Mahalik
Mr. Hani Masri
Oehme, van Sweden & Associates, Inc.
Mrs. Charles W. Scarborough
Mr. Victor Shargai
Mr. Robert M. Shoffner
Mr. John M. Steward, Jr.
Mr. Richard L. Storch
Peggy Lane Temple
Grace Weitman
Mr. O. M. Wellslager, Jr.
Mr. and Mrs. Carl D. Whitman

CONTRIBUTORS TO THE TRACY TORREY GARDEN FUND

Mr. Allan D. Angerio
Mr. John F. Duff
Mr. and Mrs. Barker Torrey
Mr. and Mrs. Barker Torrey, Jr.
Miss Beverly Torrey
Mr. and Mrs. Gordon Torrey
Transportation Department,
Plymouth County Sheriff's Department,
Plymouth, Massachusetts
Dr. Rocco J. Volpe
Mr. C. D. Whitman
Mr. Richard A. Woody

BLAIR HOUSE CONTRIBUTORS

Mrs. Barbara Adams
Mr. and Mrs. Jamar Adcock
Mrs. John Alison
Mr. Richard G. Allen
Miss Sharon Allen
Mr. and Mrs. James Alsdorf
Mrs. Susan Mary Alsop
Mr. and Mrs. Walter James Amoss
Miss Julie Andrews
Colonel and Mrs. William J. Ankley
Mr. and Mrs. Eugene Aschaffenburg
Mr. and Mrs. Joseph Aschheim
Mr. Jarvis Astaire
Mr. and Mrs. Douglas Auchincloss
Miss Sarah Avellar
Mr. and Mrs. Malcolm Baldrige
Mr. Marshall Ballard, Jr.
Mrs. Libba Barnes
Mr. and Mrs. Thomas G. Bartnick
Mr. Lucius D. Battle
Mr. Randell Baumgardner
Mrs. Jeanne Viner Bell
Mr. and Mrs. Howard Bender
Mr. and Mrs. Morton A. Bender
Mrs. Louise G. Bennett
Miss Jayne A. Bennett

Mr. Frank S. Benson, Jr.
Mr. and Mrs. Tom Benson
Mrs. Jean C. Bergaust
Wilma and Stuart A. Bernstein
Mr. and Mrs. C. Richard Beyda
Mr. Mark Biedlingmaier
Miss Armande Billion
Mr. and Mrs. William McCormick Blair, Jr.
Mr. and Mrs. Stuart Marshall Bloch
Mr. and Mrs. Huntington T. Block
Mrs. Edwin Blum
Mr. Harry J. Blumenthal, Jr.
Mrs. Joan Benny Blumofe
Mr. and Mrs. Robert Bolton
Mrs. Walter Bolton
Mr. and Mrs. Arnaud de Borchgrave
Mrs. Lois Bozilov
Mr. and Mrs. John de Braganca
Mr. and Mrs. Kenneth Broadwell
Mr. and Mrs. Raymond C. Brophy
Mrs. Dean E. Brown, Jr.
Mr. and Mrs. Donald A. Brown
Mrs. Douglas C. Brown
Mrs. Royall Brown
Mrs. Louise M. Brunsdale
Mrs. Aliki M. Bryant
Mrs. Wiley T. Buchanan III
Mr. and Mrs. Dean Burch
Mr. and Mrs. Morris Burka
Mrs. Poe Burling
Mr. and Mrs. Henry Burr
Sergeant and Mrs. Michael H. Bye
Mr. and Mrs. Robert Bye
Mr. and Mrs. Sammy Cahn
Miss Chenobia Calhoun
Dr. Mark W. Cannon
Mr. and Mrs. Carlo Capomazza di Campolattaro
Mr. and Mrs. Oliver T. Carr
Mr. and Mrs. W. Plack Carr
Mr. and Mrs. Ernest A. Carrere, Jr.
Mr. Walter Carroll, Jr.
Mrs. Hodding Carter
Mr. and Mrs. Eugene Carusi
Mr. and Mrs. Albert V. Casey
Mrs. Turner Catledge
Mr. Aldus H. Chapin
Mr. and Mrs. John E. Chapoton
Mr. and Mrs. Walter F. Chappell III
Mrs. Mary M. Chewning
Mr. and Mrs. Blair Childs
Mr. and Mrs. James A. Churchill
Mrs. Sallie Claibourn
Mrs. Mary A. Clark
Mr. and Mrs. William P. Clark
Mr. and Mrs. Robert L. Clarke
Mr. and Mrs. William R. Codus
Mr. and Mrs. Henry R. Cohen
Mr. and Mrs. Melvin S. Cohen
Mr. and Mrs. Richard S. Cohen
Mrs. Shirlie Cohen
Mr. and Mrs. Martin C. Cole
Mr. and Mrs. James J. Coleman
Mr. and Mrs. James J. Coleman, Jr.
Mr. and Mrs. Clement E. Conger
Mr. and Mrs. J. Michael Cook
Mr. and Mrs. Jack Coopersmith
Mr. and Mrs. Joseph Coors
Mr. and Mrs. William Coors
Mrs. Jane Gordon Coyne
Mr. Marshall Coyne
Mrs. Dorothy Crosby
Mr. and Mrs. George P. Crounse
Mr. and Mrs. Charles Cudlip

Dr. and Mrs. H. Tucker Dalton
Mr. Patrick J. Daly
Mrs. Virginia Warren Daly
Mrs. Ethel E. Danzansky
Mr. Joseph Davenport III
Mr. and Mrs. Walter Davis
Mrs. Mona Dearborn
Mr. and Mrs. Michael K. Deaver
Mrs. Amalia Lacroze de Fortabat
Mrs. Charles de Limur
Mr. and Mrs. George Denegre
Ms. Patricia Devine
Mr. and Mrs. Morse Dial
Mr. and Mrs. Richard E. Diamond
Dr. and Mrs. Walter Diaz
Mr. and Mrs. Charles J. DiBona
Mr. and Mrs. C. Mathews Dick
Ms. Pat Dixson
Mr. and Mrs. William T. Dooley
Mr. and Mrs. Robert Dowler
Mr. Richard F. Driscoll
Mr. and Mrs. Angier Biddle Duke
Mr. George Dunbar
Mr. and Mrs. Brooke H. Duncan II
Mr. and Mrs. Lawrence Dunham
Mrs. Kathleen Bryan Edwards
Mrs. Elizabeth Mize Elicker
Mrs. Elizabeth Jane Elliott
Mrs. Charles W. Engelhard
Mr. and Mrs. Melvyn J. Estrin
Mr. and Mrs. A. Huda Farouki
Mr. and Mrs. Aspy Fataki
Mrs. J. Morgan Fauth
Mr. and Mrs. D. Blair Favrot
Mr. and Mrs. William Feltus
Mrs. Darwin S. Fenner
Mr. and Mrs. James L. Ferguson
Mr. Marc A. Ferrara
Mr. Simon C. Fireman

Mr. and Mrs. Leonard K. Firestone
Mr. and Mrs. Ashton Fischer
Mrs. J. Clifford Folger
Mr. and Mrs. Lee M. Folger
Mr. Christopher Forbes
Mr. Malcolm S. Forbes, Sr.
The Forest Fund
Foundation for Middle East Peace
Mrs. Yolande B. Fox
Mr. and Mrs. Louis Freeman

Mr. Richard A. Freling
Mr. and Mrs. F. Charles Froelicher
Mr. and Mrs. Evan G. Galbraith
Mr. and Mrs. Francesco Galesi
Mr. and Mrs. Roger Gant, Jr.
Mr. and Mrs. John D. Garner
Mr. and Mrs. Charles Gates
Mrs. Mabel Connor Gerardi
Miss Marie Catherine Gerardi
Mr. and Mrs. Joseph Gildenhorn
Ms. Christina Ginsburg
Mr. and Mrs. Stanley Glassman
Mr. and Mrs. Frank Godchaux
Mrs. Maidie B. Goddard
Mr. and Mrs. Terence C. Golden
Mr. and Mrs. H. Hunter Goodrich
Mr. and Mrs. Richard Gookin
Mr. Bernard Gordon
Mr. and Mrs. MacKenzie Gordon
Mr. and Mrs. H. D. Graham
Mr. and Mrs. Gilbert Greenway
Mr. and Mrs. Frederick Haack
Mr. Richard O. Haase
Mr. and Mrs. Lloyd N. Hand
Mr. and Mrs. David G. Hanes
Mrs. Frank B. Hanes
Mr. and Mrs. Gordon Hanes
Mr. and Mrs. Philip Hanes
Mrs. B. Lauriston Hardin
Mrs. Verna Harrah
Mrs. Joseph Haspel
The HCA Foundation
Mr. and Mrs. Richard W. Heath
Mr. and Mrs. John O. Hedden
Mr. and Mrs. Henry J. Heinz II
Senator and Mrs. John Heinz
Mr. and Mrs. Joseph H. Hennage
Mr. Christian A. Herter, Jr.
Mrs. Dorothy Gordon Heyser
Mr. John S. Hilson
Mrs. Walter J. Hodges
Mrs. William Hodges
Miss Barbara Lynn Hornor
Mr. J. Henry Hoskinson
Dr. Richard Howland
Mr. and Mrs. Michael Huffington
Mr. and Mrs. Killian Huger
Ms. Caroline Rose Hunt
Mr. and Mrs. Frank Ikard
Mr. and Mrs. Bronson Ingram
Institute of International Education
Mr. and Mrs. Robert Livingston Ireland III
Mrs. Jean Jackson
Mr. and Mrs. Erik Johnsen
Mrs. Charles B. Johnson
Mr. and Mrs. Lloyd Johnson
Mr. and Mrs. H. Bradley Jones
Mr. and Mrs. Earle Jorgensen
Mr. and Mrs. Jack Josey
Mr. and Mrs. James Kabler
Mr. Robert Kaiser
Mr. and Mrs. Ford A. Kalil, Jr.
Mrs. Garfield Kass
Mr. and Mrs. Marvin Kay
Bishop and Mrs. Christoph Keller, Jr.
Mr. Thomas Keller
Mrs. Katherine Kelley
Dr. and Mrs. Eamon Kelly
Mr. and Mrs. William H. Kent
Mr. and Mrs. Robert Kerrigan, Jr.
Mr. and Mrs. Harold M. Keshishian
Mr. and Mrs. James M. Keshishian
Mrs. Randolph A. Kidder

Mr. William C. Killgallon
Dr. Henry A. Kissinger
Mr. and Mrs. Herbert W. Klotz
Mr. and Mrs. E. James Kock, Jr.
Dr. Virginia Kock
Mr. and Mrs. Daniel Korengold
Mr. and Mrs. Thomas E. Korengold
Mr. and Mrs. Fred Korth
Mr. and Mrs. Fritz-Alan Korth
Mr. Peter Kovler
Ms. Susan Cullman Kudlow
Mr. and Mrs. Dimitrios Kyriakopoulos
Mr. and Mrs. John P. Labouisse
Mr. Hillyer Speed Lamkin
Mr. and Mrs. Robert D. Largey, Sr.
Mr. and Mrs. Climis G. Lascaris
Senator and Mrs. Paul Laxalt
Ms. Cynthia D. Lee
Colonel E. Brooke Lee, Jr.
Mr. Samuel Lehrman
Mr. Marc E. Leland
Mr. and Mrs. Thomas B. Lemann
Mr. and Mrs. Eugene Lewis
Mr. Vince Lewis
Mr. and Mrs. Raymond H. Lilly, Jr.
Mr. and Mrs. Mark Littman
Mrs. Henry Malcolm Lloyd
Dr. and Mrs. Samuel Logan
Mr. and Mrs. John H. Lollar III
Mrs. Eugene A. Lundgren
Mr. and Mrs. Edwin Lupberger
Mrs. Charles F. Lynch
Ms. Linda McCausland

Mr. and Mrs. William McCollam
Mr. and Mrs. Dermot McGlinchey
Mr. and Mrs. Earl McGowin
Mrs. Julian McGowin
Dr. and Mrs. Armand McHenry
Mrs. Edmund McIlhenny
Mrs. Juliette Clagett McLennan
Mr. and Mrs. Martin F. Malarkey
Mrs. Carolyn J. Maness
Margaret Dorrance Strawbridge Foundation
of Pennsylvania II, Inc.
The Marks Foundation, Inc.
Mr. and Mrs. Michael Marsiglia
Mr. and Mrs. Reuben David Martinez
Mr. and Mrs. William Marvel
Mr. and Mrs. John D. Mashek, Jr.

Ms. Mary Masserini
Mr. and Mrs. Charles B. Mayer
Mr. and Mrs. Joseph Mele
Mr. and Mrs. Kenneth F. Melley
Mr. and Mrs. William R. Merriam
Mr. and Mrs. Charles A. Meyer
Mr. and Mrs. George S. Michals
Miss Alexandra G. Miller
Mr. and Mrs. Gary W. Miller
Mrs. Judith Miller
Mr. and Mrs. Paul C. Miller
The Milton Company
Mr. and Mrs. George R. Montgomery
Mr. and Mrs. Richard H. Moore
Mr. and Mrs. Edmund Morris
Mr. and Mrs. Emil Mosbacher, Jr.
Mr. and Mrs. Robert Mosbacher, Sr.
Mount Vernon Club, Inc.
Mr. and Mrs. Patrick N. Munroe
Miss Catherine Murdock
Mr. and Mrs. Donald Nalty
Mr. and Mrs. Bernard N. Neal, Jr.
Mrs. Isidore Newman II
Mr. and Mrs. Jerry Nicholson
Mr. and Mrs. Thomas H. Nimick, Jr.
Mrs. Fernanda Niven
Mr. Gerson Nordlinger, Jr.
Count and Countess Christoph Nostitz
Mr. and Mrs. A. J. Nugon
Mr. and Mrs. John D. Ochs
Mrs. John Ochsner
Mr. and Mrs. Frederick W. O'Green
Dr. and Mrs. Martin O'Neill, Jr.
Mr. and Mrs. W. McKerrall O'Neill, Jr.
Mrs. Alfred M. Osgood
Mr. and Mrs. George O'Sullivan
Mr. and Mrs. Robert B. Ourisman
Mrs. Dudley Owen
Dr. and Mrs. John Q. Owsley, Jr.
Mr. and Mrs. Stanley C. Pace
Mr. and Mrs. Walter Parlange, Jr.
Mrs. Carol Layton Parsons
Mr. and Mrs. Gordon B. Pattee
Mrs. Francis E. Pearson III
Colonel and Mrs. Edouard A. Peloquin
Mr. and Mrs. John J. Pendergast III
Mr. and Mrs. Robert L. Pettit, Jr.
Mr. Roy Pfautch
Mr. and Mrs. John E. Pflieger
Mr. and Mrs. Sumner Pingree III
Ms. Zenda L. Pipkin
Mr. Paul S. Plauche
Ms. Jane E. Powell
Mr. and Mrs. Peter Pratt
Dr. and Mrs. Jerold J. Principato
Ms. Dona L. Proctor
Mr. and Mrs. Norman S. Rabb
Mrs. Nigel Rafferty
Mrs. Donna Lee Rautbord
Mr. and Mrs. Charles S. Reily
Mr. and Mrs. Robert Reisfeld
Mr. and Mrs. A. William Reynolds
Mrs. Richard S. Reynolds, Jr.
Mr. Rex Rice
Mrs. Francoise Richardson
Mrs. Walter Ridder
Renah Blair Rietzke Family Foundation
Mrs. Beedy T. Ritchie
Dr. Frank Rizza
Mrs. Geoffrey Roberts, M.B.E.
Dr. and Mrs. George A. Roberts
Mr. and Mrs. Gilbert A. Robinson
Mr. and Mrs. Samuel G. Robinson

Mrs. Stuart Rockwell
Mr. Cornelius Van S. Roosevelt
Mrs. Arthur R. Rose
Mr. and Mrs. James S. Rosebush
Mr. and Mrs. Robert M. Rosenthal
Dr. and Mrs. Herbert B. Rothschild
Mr. and Mrs. John H. Rousselot
Mr. and Mrs. Dean Rusk
Mr. and Mrs. John Russos
Miss Sana T. Sabbagh
Mr. E. Harold Saer, Jr.
Dr. and Mrs. J. Kenneth Saer
Mrs. Stanley Sarnoff
Miss Norna S. Sarofim
Mr. and Mrs. George T. Scharffenberger
Mr. and Mrs. Lee H. Schlesinger
Mrs. Robert A. Schulman
Mr. and Mrs. Richard A. Schuman
Mr. and Mrs. James P. Schwartz, Jr.
Mrs. Farol Seretean
Mrs. Charles H. Sethness, Jr.
Mr. Henry B. Sethness
Mr. and Mrs. Edward Seymour, Jr.
Miss Irene Shortley
Mrs. Najla Showker
Mrs. Peter Sideris
Mrs. John Farr Simmons
Mr. Harold Simmons
Mr. and Mrs. Henry Singleton
Ms. Donna Sirko
Mr. and Mrs. Sanford Slavin
Mr. and Mrs. Earl F. Slick
Mrs. Jane DeGraff Sloat
Mr. and Mrs. Albert H. Small
Mrs. Joyce Small
Mr. and Mrs. John B. Smallpage
Mr. George P. Smith II
Mr. Gerard C. Smith
Mr. and Mrs. Robert N. Snyder
Miss Katherine Sotiropoulos
Mr. and Mrs. Patrick Sotiropoulos
Mrs. Frederick Stafford
Mr. and Mrs. Julian Steinberg
Mrs. McDonald Stephens
Mr. and Mrs. Edgar B. Stern, Jr.
Mr. and Mrs. George Stevens, Jr.
Mr. and Mrs. Edward L. Stone
Mr. James H. Stone
Mrs. Roger T. Stone
Mr. and Mrs. Frank Strachan
Mrs. Joy Sundlun
Mrs. Catherine H. Sweeny
Mr. and Mrs. James W. Symington
Mrs. Deborah Szekely
Mrs. Mae Sue Talley
Mr. Michael Tarver
Mr. and Mrs. Patrick Taylor
Mr. and Mrs. Macy O. Teetor, Jr.
Mr. and Mrs. Liener Temerlin
Mr. and Mrs. Daniel J. Terra
Miss Mary E. Testa
Mr. N. O. Thomas, Jr.
Mr. and Mrs. Merle Thorpe, Jr.
Mr. Timothy L. Towell
Mr. and Mrs. Middleton Train
Mr. and Mrs. Thomas W. Trainer
Mr. and Mrs. Morrell Trimble
Mr. and Mrs. Eli Tullis
Mr. Michael Valentine
Mrs. Benedicte Valentiner
Mrs. Maryellen Vandivier
Mrs. Robert D. van Roijen
Mr. and Mrs. Frank Voelker, Jr.

Arthur and Janet Ross Garden. Janet Ross, 1988.

Blair House Dining Room.

Photography Credits:
Kari Haavisto: front cover, pages 34, 34-35, 42, 43, 50, 51, 52, 55, 58, 59, 62-63, 64, 65, 66, 76, 77, and 78. Hickey-Robertson: pages 2, 4-5, 8, 31, 46, 47, 49, 53, 54, 60, 70, 72-73, 74, and 80. Mary E. Nichols: pages 1, 6-7, 32-33, 36-37, 38, 38-39, 40-41, 44-45, 48, 56-57, 61, 66-67, 68-69, and 70-71. John F. Grant: page 10.

Photography by Hickey-Robertson, courtesy of *Southern Accents,* Southern Progress Corporation. Photography by Mary E. Nichols, courtesy of *Architectural Digest,* copyright © 1988 Architectural Digest Publishing Corporation. All rights reserved.

Archival Photography and Illustration Credits:
Pages 12, 15, 17, 22, and 23 courtesy of the Rare Book and Special Collections Division, Library of Congress, Washington, D.C. Page 18 courtesy of St. John's Church, Washington, D.C. Page 20 courtesy of Decatur House, a property of the National Trust for Historic Preservation. Page 26 courtesy of The National Portrait Gallery, Smithsonian Institution, Gift of Dr. Montgomery Blair. Pages 27 and 28 copyright © *Washington Post*. Reprinted by permission of the D.C. Public Library. Page 29 Associated Press. Page 30 and back cover courtesy of Washingtoniana Division, D.C. Public Library. Page 79 courtesy of Janet Ross.

Interior Decoration Credits:
Mario Buatta: pages 6-7, 40-41, 48-55, 60-61, 66-74, 76, 77, and 78. Mark Hampton: front cover, pages 4-5, 8, 31-39, 44-47, 56-59, 62-65, and 80.